BIZARRE BIRDS

BY LIBBY WILSON

Apex is distributed by North Star Editions:
sales@northstareditions.com | 888-417-0195

Produced for Apex by Red Line Editorial.

Photographs ©: Shutterstock Images, cover, 1, 4–5, 6, 6–7, 8–9, 10–11, 12, 14, 15, 16–17, 19, 20–21, 22–23, 24–25, 26, 29; Nature Picture Library/Alamy, 13; Neil Bowman/Alamy, 18

Library of Congress Control Number: 2022919858

ISBN
978-1-63738-527-2 (hardcover)
978-1-63738-581-4 (paperback)
978-1-63738-688-0 (ebook pdf)
978-1-63738-635-4 (hosted ebook)

Printed in the United States of America
Mankato, MN
082023

NOTE TO PARENTS AND EDUCATORS

Apex books are designed to build literacy skills in striving readers. Exciting, high-interest content attracts and holds readers' attention. The text is carefully leveled to allow students to achieve success quickly. Additional features, such as bolded glossary words for difficult terms, help build comprehension.

TABLE OF CONTENTS

CHAPTER 1

WILD FLYERS

Afrigate bird **soars** over the ocean. The large bird has been flying for weeks. It is very hungry. Suddenly, it spots a seagull.

A frigate bird can fly for up to eight weeks without stopping.

The frigate bird swoops to attack. But it doesn't eat the gull. Instead, it bites the gull's tail and shakes.

Frigate birds sometimes steal food from other birds.

By soaring on winds high in the sky, frigate birds don't have to flap their wings as often.

LONG FLIGHT

Frigate birds are seabirds. But they cannot swim. Instead, they fly long distances. Many frigate birds **migrate** across oceans. To save energy, the birds soar on winds high in the sky.

The scared seagull throws up. The frigate bird eats the **vomit**. Then it keeps flying to look for more food.

A frigate bird can travel thousands of miles. It catches fish to eat along the way.

FAST FACT

A frigate bird sleeps while flying. Half the bird's brain sleeps at a time.

CHAPTER 2

UNUSUAL FOODS

Some birds have strange diets. Marabou storks are **scavengers**. They often eat trash. Some even eat metal or human waste.

Marabou storks often eat dead animals.

Kea can hurt sheep, so many people hunted them. Today, kea are in danger of dying out.

Kea are parrots that live in New Zealand. They sometimes attack sheep. The birds land on a sheep's back. They use their beaks to tear off chunks of wool and meat.

Vampire finches live on the Galápagos Islands.

Bearded vultures can eat bones that are up to 10 inches (25 cm) long.

Bearded vultures mainly eat bones. They swallow small bones whole. They drop large bones from the sky. The bones smash on rocks. Vultures can then eat the **marrow** inside.

FEATHER PROTECTION

Some grebes eat their own feathers. The feathers trap sharp parts of the birds' food. They form balls. Grebes spit these balls back up.

Eared grebes often eat shrimp and insects.

CHAPTER 3

STRANGE MATES

Many male birds show off to attract **mates**. Resplendent quetzals grow long tails. Their tails can be 3 feet (1 m) long.

A male resplendent quetzal's tail can be twice as long as his body.

When it is not dancing, a superb bird of paradise keeps its black feathers folded up.

Superb birds of paradise change shape. Males spread their feathers wide. They look like dinner plates with faces. Then males dance around females.

Only adult male Costa's hummingbirds flare their feathers.

FAST FACT

Costa's hummingbirds **flare** feathers on their faces. The feathers look like an octopus.

After the mating dance, a female greater prairie chicken chooses one male to mate with.

Greater prairie chickens do a group dance. Up to 70 males may take part. The birds drum their feet. They leap and kick.

BIG BOOMS

Male greater prairie chickens have air sacs on their throats. Males **inflate** these sacs as they dance. They make a loud booming sound. It can be heard 1 mile (1.6 km) away.

CHAPTER 4

WEiRDEST NESTS

Sociable weavers build enormous nests. One nest can weigh as much as a small car. It may hold up to 500 birds. Each bird pair has its own room.

Sociable weavers make their nests from straw, grass, and twigs.

Mallee fowl build mounds of sticks, leaves, and sand. The mounds can be 9 feet (3 m) wide. Females lay eggs inside them. Chicks hatch several weeks later.

THE RIGHT TEMPERATURE

Mallee fowl dads keep the eggs at 91 degrees Fahrenheit (33ºC). They dig air holes in hot weather. They add sand when it's cold.

Mallee fowl usually lay about 15 to 30 eggs in each mound.

Female hornbills lay eggs in hollow trees. Then they cover the openings with poop and vomit. Mothers and chicks stay inside for up to four months.

FAST FACT

The male hornbill passes food through a small slit. The slit also acts as a toilet.

The male hornbill brings food to the nest for its family to eat.

COMPREHENSION QUESTIONS

Write your answers on a separate piece of paper.

1. Write a few sentences describing one way male birds show off to attract mates.

2. Which bird described in the book would you most like to see in real life? Why?

3. Which type of bird mainly eats bones?

    A. vampire finch

    B. bearded vulture

    C. grebe

4. Why would mallee fowl dads keep their mounds a certain temperature?

    A. so the mounds feel nice to sit on

    B. so the eggs can stay safe and grow

    C. so female mallee fowl will stay away

5. What does **diets** mean in this book?

*Some birds have strange **diets**. Marabou storks are scavengers. They often eat trash.*

    A. the size an animal usually grows

    B. the places an animal usually lives

    C. the things an animal usually eats

6. What does **enormous** mean in this book?

*Sociable weavers build **enormous** nests. One nest can weigh as much as a small car.*

    A. very big

    B. very small

    C. not real

Answer key on page 32.

GLOSSARY

flare

To make something stand up or stick out.

inflate

To puff up by filling with air.

marrow

Soft, fatty material in the center of bones.

mates

Pairs of animals that come together to have babies.

migrate

To move from one part of the world to another.

scavengers

Animals that eat whatever they can find, such as garbage and dead things.

soars

Flies high in the air without flapping wings very often.

vomit

The bits of food and juices that are thrown up.

TO LEARN MORE

BOOKS

Jackson, Tom. *The Magnificent Book of Birds.* San Rafael, CA: Weldon Owen, 2021.

Shaffer, Lindsay. *Bearded Vultures.* Minneapolis: Bellwether Media, 2020.

Unwin, Cyndy. *Birds of Paradise: Winged Wonders.* New York: Children's Press, 2020.

ONLINE RESOURCES

Visit **www.apexeditions.com** to find links and resources related to this title.

ABOUT THE AUTHOR

Libby Wilson loves birds. Chickadees sit on her head while she fills their feeder, she calls to owls on winter nights, and she longs to see a bird of paradise someday.

INDEX

ANSWER KEY:
1. Answers will vary; 2. Answers will vary; 3. B; 4. B; 5. C; 6. A